Thirty Days of Thanksgiving

A Devotional for Personal and Small Group Use During

Any Season of the Year

By: Jeremy G. Woods

Published by:
FaithVenture Media
Târgu Mureş, România

Thirty Days of Thanksgiving: A Devotional for Personal and
Small Group Use During Any Season of the Year
Written by: Jeremy G. Woods
Copyright © 2017 by Jeremy G. Woods

FaithVenture Media - *www.faithventuremedia.com*
Târgu Mureş, România

"But without faith it is impossible to please Him, for he who
comes to God must believe that He is, and that He is a rewarder
of those who diligently seek Him." Hebrews 11:6 NKJV

Descrierea CIP a Bibliotecii Naţionale a României
WOODS, JEREMY G.
   Thirty days of thanksgiving : a devotional for personal and
small group use during any season of the year / Jeremy G.
Woods. - Târgu Mureş : FaithVenture Media, 2017
   ISBN 978-606-94447-2-6

2

Scripture taken from the *New King James Version®*. Copyright
© 1982 by Thomas Nelson. Used by permission. All rights
reserved.

Other Works by Jeremy G. Woods

In Peril's Way (2009, 2011) – May become a mystery series

Fun and Easy Ways to Learn French (2011)

The Missing Ingredient in Our Prayer Life (2012)

Go For It! Motivating Christians to Do God's Will (2013)

Faith Without Borders (2015)

Using Technology for Your Church (2017)

To see more about Jeremy's and his wife's books and updates, visit their website at:
www.jeremyandmagdawoods.com

To see the web page for this book, visit
www.faithventuremedia.com/thirty-days-of-thanksgiving

Jeremy's wife, Magda, just published her debut novel entitled "Providence: God's Care for the Lost Sheep." You can find more info at
www.faithventuremedia.com/providence

Books Published by FaithVenture Media

Using Technology for Your Church (2017)

Providence: God's Care for the Lost Sheep (2017)

Thirty Days of Thanksgiving (2017)

To find out more about FaithVenture Media, visit

www.faithventuremedia.com

Table of Contents

Dedication

This book is dedicated to God, as I live to serve and please Him. My hope and prayer are that He will use this book to help Church members and Churches keep a focus on thanksgiving year-round.

This book is also dedicated to my wife, Magda. She is a great helpmate for me, and I am very thankful to have her in my life, during all of the life's ups and downs. I look forward to writing more books with her help and encouragement and to encourage her as she is also writing.

I am very thankful for all the people who have endorsed this book and supported it in any way. For those in our Writing Advocacy Facebook group, I would like to especially thank them as they seek ways to help Magda and me promote our Christian books.

How to Use This Book

This book is meant to be read one page a day for a month. Each day's reading starts with a Bible verse or a small Bible passage (each one based on the topic of thanksgiving). There is a short exposition on the verse or on a topic of the verse or passage. There are also three questions each day for you to ponder.

There is also a section at the end of the book to allow this book to be used for small group discussions. As mentioned in the back, when using this book for small groups, I have divided the topics into eight weeks, so this book can be done in a two-month period for small group discussions (but the topics can be doubled up, and the study can be done in a month if needed).

Although the theme of the devotional is thanksgiving, that does not have to be the only season that you use the book. It can be done at any point in the year.

<u>Part One: Personal Devotions</u>

Today and throughout the remainder of the days that you read this book, purpose in your heart to find ways to thank the Lord. God is good all the time, so we should not cease to give Him thanksgiving. I pray that as you carefully do each devotional, you will remember to be thankful to God each day for His blessings upon us. Although each day's reading and devotional is short, use the question section of each day to ponder what you have just read.

Day 1

Psalm 100:4-5: "Enter into His gates with thanksgiving, And into His courts with praise. Be thankful to Him, and bless His name. For the Lord is good; His mercy is everlasting, And His truth endures to all generations."

Today, remember that God is good. When we go throughout our day, we should be reminded of Him and His goodness towards us. When someone doesn't treat us the way we want to be treated, remember that we were hateful towards God. However, because Jesus paid for our sins on the cross and we have chosen to walk in His grace, we will be given the grace to forgive others.

Day 1 – Questions to Ponder
1. What ways have you seen God work in your life this week?
2. How many times do you thank God each day?
3. Have you held a grudge against someone in the past week? What can you do to remove that grudge?

Day 2

> **1 Corinthians 1:4**: "I thank my God always concerning you for the grace of God which was given to you by Christ Jesus."

Spend some time in prayer and thankfulness for the Godly leaders who have influenced your life. We are not independent of each other; we are co-dependent. We have to rely on others to help us shape us into who we are to be.

Day 2 - Questions to Ponder
1. *Who influenced your life the most?*
2. *What would your life be like now without the Godly people in your past and present?*
3. *Who can you start to influence in your life right now?*

Day 3

> **2 Timothy 1:5:** "...When I call to remembrance the genuine faith that is in you, which dwelt first in your grandmother Lois and your mother Eunice, and I am persuaded is in you also."

Spend some time in prayer and thankfulness for the education that you had. Think back to all your former teachers and pray for them. These people have had a huge part of who you are. They have helped build you up. If you've had any good Christian mentors (including a Godly influence from your parents), also thank God for them.

Day 3 - Questions to Ponder
1. *Who was your favorite teacher?*
2. *What lessons did you get most out of your schooling?*
3. *Who can you help mentor in your life right now?*

Day 4

> **1 Timothy 2:1-4**: "You therefore, my son, be strong in the grace that is in Christ Jesus. And the things that you have heard from me among many witnesses, commit these to faithful men who will be able to teach others also. You therefore must endure hardship as a good soldier of Jesus Christ. No one engaged in warfare entangles himself with the affairs of this life, that he may please him who enlisted him as a soldier."

Take time to pray for and thank God for your country's leaders. Our world is in a critical period of history. Pray that your country's leaders will become faithful to God and that God will send a revival to your country's government.

Day 4 - Questions to Ponder

1. *How can you best get involved in your government?*
2. *How studied up are you in current events?*
3. *How can you reach your local leaders for Christ?*

Day 5

> **Ephesians 5:33**: "Nevertheless let each one of you in particular so love his own wife as himself, and let the wife see that she respects her husband."

Thank God for your spouse, if you are married, or thank God for and pray for your future spouse if you are not married. God has ordained marriage as a symbol of His relationship to us. Since marriage is not to be taken lightly, make it a point to put effort into your relationship. This should really be a daily thing, not just something to do on Day 5 while you're doing this devotional.

Day 5 - Questions to Ponder
1. How can you show love to your spouse today?
2. How often do you write your spouse a love letter? Can you write one today for your spouse or future spouse?
3. What do you admire most about your spouse? Tell him or her today.

Day 6

> **Proverbs 17:17**: "A friend loves at all times, And a brother is born for adversity."

Thank God for your friends. Good friends can be hard to find, so thank God for the ones you have. Jesus' disciples were His friends, His main friends that He had on this earth. Although one of them betrayed Him and the rest forsook Him when He died on the cross, Jesus' friends did love Him, and He loved His friends and died on the cross for them. In fact, Jesus says that we are His friends if we hear Him and do what He says. Thank Jesus that He is your friend, and thank Him for showing the ultimate sacrifice to bring you to repentance and restoration to God.

Day 6 - Questions to Ponder
1. *Who are your friends?*
2. *Are you showing yourself to be a good friend to your own friends?*
3. *Are you thankful for Jesus' friendship?*

Day 7

> **Philippians 4:6**: "Be anxious for nothing, but in everything by prayer and supplication, with thanksgiving, let your requests be made known to God."

Be thankful that you don't have to be worried. Also, be grateful that God has everything under control. He's the Alpha and Omega, the Beginning and the End. He created it all, and He allows us to come before Him when we have problems. He doesn't say, "Come only between these particular times of the day," or "Don't come – I'm on vacation." He is available during the day, during the night, and He speaks your language. He understands what has happened to you, and He is able to do anything. With such a God like Him, how can we not be thankful, even in our worst situations, that He is available to take care of all our worries?

Day 7 - Questions to Ponder
1. *When have you last thanked God for who He is?*
2. *What problems are you now facing that you haven't thought to bring before God's throne?*
3. *Do you truly believe that God can bring you out of your situations?*

Day 8

> **Philippians 4:8:** "Finally, brethren, whatever things are true, whatever things are noble, whatever things are just, whatever things are pure, whatever things are lovely, whatever things are of good report, if there is any virtue and if there is anything praiseworthy—meditate on these things."

What has been good in your life lately? Think about all your blessings, and thank God for them. Instead of thinking about everything that might have been going wrong in your life lately, try focusing on the good things. Yes, sometimes, we tend to focus on the bad, but that usually brings us down. God wants us to be grateful for the good things He's given us and to give Him all our worries.

Day 8 - Questions to Ponder
1. *What blessings has God given you lately?*
2. *How often do you focus on the bad in life rather than the good?*
3. *How can you give God all your worries?*

Day 9

Psalm 50:14: "Offer to God thanksgiving, And pay your vows to the Most High."

God deserves all our thanks. He also deserves us to pay any vows we have made Him. If we have told God that if He does something for us (e.g. help us with something) that we would do something for Him and He has done what we asked, the Bible says that we are to fulfill our vows that we made to God. During this time, if you can recall any time that you've made a vow to God during your life, you need to pay the vow. A vow is a serious thing, and it is a debt (just like thanksgiving) that we owe to God if we have made a vow.

Day 9 - Questions to Ponder
1. Have you made a vow to God?
2. If so, what will it take to pay God back?
3. Has God helped you through difficult situations, even ones where you did not make a vow to God? Thank Him for His provision for you.

Day 10

> **Hebrews 13:5:** *"Let your* conduct *be* without covetousness; *be* content with such things as you have. For He Himself has said, 'I will never leave you nor forsake you.'"*

The Bible is clear that we should be content with what we have. What you have is a blessing from God, and if you are not content with it, then you are ungrateful, which is the opposite of being thankful. We deserve an ultimate punishment for our sins, but because of God's goodness, we have an opportunity to spend forever in Heaven with Him.

Heaven is not something that we deserve. Therefore, our focus should be thanksgiving for what God has blessed us with, and we should not become upset when we see others have things we don't have. In fact, not coveting is one of the Ten Commandments. "You shall not covet ... anything that *is* your neighbor's" (**Exodus 20:17**).

Day 10 - Questions to Ponder
1. *Have you been coveting something that someone has lately?*
2. *Are you grateful for what God has given you?*
3. *If you have been ungrateful, have you asked God forgiveness for an ungrateful heart? If not, do so now.*

Day 11

> **Psalm 26:6-8:** "I will wash my hands in innocence; So I will go about Your altar, O Lord, That I may proclaim with the voice of thanksgiving, And tell of all Your wondrous works. Lord, I have loved the habitation of Your house, And the place where Your glory dwells."

God doesn't dwell in temples; the Holy Spirit lives inside those who are saved by God. Even though we meet as a Church on Sundays and whenever else our congregation meets, God is with us anywhere we go. However, there still is something special about God's presence while we meet at our Church congregations. We should be thankful for the times we get to worship God with other Christians, sing praises to Him, and hear His Word preached from our Pastor.

God lives in each of us as Christians, so this should bring us hope and love for others that we couldn't have on our own. The Creator of the world works through us and wants us to share about His goodness to others around us. Isn't this good news?

Day 11 - Questions to Ponder
1. *Have you asked God for forgiveness lately?*
2. *Do you love attending Church?*
3. *What would make your experience at Church better?*

Day 12

> **Psalm 9:1:** "I will praise *You,* O LORD, with my whole heart; I will tell of all Your marvelous works."

We aren't just supposed to love God partly, but with all our being. Jesus was asked what the greatest commandment was, and He said, "Jesus said to him, "'You shall love the LORD your God with all your heart, with all your soul, and with all your mind.' This is *the* first and great commandment. And *the* second *is* like it: 'You shall love your neighbor as yourself'"" (**Matthew 22:37-39**).

This is a commandment but also something that happens as we learn to trust God more. Our trials are one way that God builds our faith in Him. We can think of these trials like a test from when we were in school. Tests were ways that the teacher could see how we apply what we learned in class. When we go through trials in life, these are ways that God can see how we apply what He has taught us. They also are in place to build our trust in Him because, when we are in situations impossible for us, that's when He's able to step in and show that He can do things that we can't imagine possible.

Day 12 - Questions to Ponder
1. *How much do you love God?*
2. *What trials have you had recently?*
3. *In what ways have you seen yourself closer to God through these trials?*

Day 13

Colossians 3:17: "And whatever you do in word or deed, *do* all in the name of the Lord Jesus, giving thanks to God the Father through Him."

The Bible says that everything we do should be done for Him. Why is this? It's because of the implications that happened at the cross. Yes, we were forgiven when Jesus died on the cross, but something else happened. Jesus' perfect life became our life, and our life was given to Jesus. It was a transfer of punishments.

Jesus did nothing wrong, but He was crucified on the cross. He stayed on the cross not because He couldn't find a way down. He stayed to take your and my punishment and to give us His life. Today, be thankful for what Jesus did for you, taking your sin and giving you His life in exchange. Also, be sure to do everything in honor of The One who gave you His life.

Day 13 - Questions to Ponder
1. How can you give Jesus honor today?
2. What does it mean to you that Jesus took your life and in exchange gave you His?
3. What are you thankful for today that God has done in your life?

Day 14

Psalm 147:7: "Sing to the LORD with thanksgiving; Sing praises on the harp to our God."

The Bible mentions instruments and singing as a way of expressing ourselves to God, the harp being mentioned a lot. God is honored in many ways, but He seems to especially like singing as a big expression of joy, praise, and thanksgiving. As soon as you can, find a song that you would like to sing to God and either play it on an instrument and sing it or just sing it to God acapella. Either way brings glory to God.

If you like to compose music, you might also try writing a praise song to God. Even if you haven't done so before, just try it. It's another way we can give God thanks. It doesn't have to be a song you show anyone else. God is praised even when we worship Him when no one else is around, and He mentions in the Bible a lot, especially in the Psalms, that we should sing new songs for Him.

Day 14 - Questions to Ponder
1. *How does singing praises to God bring Him glory?*
2. *Do you enjoy creating praise songs to God? Why or why not?*
3. *In what other ways can you bring God praise today?*

Day 15

> **1 Timothy 6:17:** "Command those who are rich in this present age not to be haughty, nor to trust in uncertain riches but in the living God, who gives us richly all things to enjoy."

Our personal wealth is not certain in this life. One moment it may be there, and another it is not there. We shouldn't put our trust in money, time, or other earthly things. Our trust should be in God, and God alone.

God is not glorified if we trust in our money but also claim to trust in Him. Our reliance on God should not depend on how much money we have or who we are. Those who are rich will have a harder time entering Heaven because Christians are supposed to rely on God and, if you have everything you need and want on earth, how can you rely on God for everything? Be thankful for what you have and ask God to help you see in which ways in life you are not thankful.

Day 15 - Questions to Ponder
1. *Are you thankful for everything God has given you?*
2. *How can you glorify God in the stage you are in?*
3. *How much do you trust God now? How can you learn to trust God more?*

Day 16

> **2 Corinthians 9:10-11:** "Now may He who supplies seed to the sower, and bread for food, supply and multiply the seed you have *sown* and increase the fruits of your righteousness, while *you are* enriched in everything for all liberality, which causes thanksgiving through us to God."

When we give to God, He rewards us. We won't see all the reward this side of Heaven, as long as our giving is in secret and not known publicly (such as through our telling others or making it public). Not only does God want you to give, but as it said in today's passage, God wants liberal giving, giving that is generous and done in excess.

When we talk about giving to God, we must first remember that He has given us everything we have. Not only has He given us everything we have, but He also gave His only begotten Son so that we can have Eternal Life. When we look at it from this perspective, then it only makes sense that we should give back to Him in thankfulness of what He has done for us. Thank God today for providing for what you need. Ask Him how you can serve Him better.

Day 16 - Questions to Ponder
1. *How is your giving?*
2. *How can you improve your giving?*
3. *Are you thankful for what you have?*

Day 17

Psalm 68:35: "O God, *You are* more awesome than Your holy places. The God of Israel *is* He who gives strength and power to *His* people. Blessed *be* God!"

God is the One who gives us strength and power when we need it (as also seen in **Isaiah 40:31**). When we need energy or strength to do something, we don't have to do it in our power. Our strength is limited, but if we pray for God to give us strength, He will take joy in doing so.

Because of this, God is worthy of our praise and thanksgiving. During this time, take the time to thank God for His provision of strength when you need it the most.

Day 17 - Questions to Ponder
1. *Has God ever given you strength when you needed it?*
2. *What do you need strength for today in your life?*
3. *Is there something that seems impossible for you now? Pray that God will work a miracle in your life and thank Him for it when He does.*

Day 18

> **1 Corinthians 1:25:** "Because the foolishness of God is wiser than men, and the weakness of God is stronger than men."

God is all-powerful. He can do anything that He wants to do, and He asks that you ask Him to do what you cannot do yourself. The Bible says that we miss out on blessings because we don't ask God for them.

Spend time thanking God for what He has provided for you. Also, pray that He will work a miracle in your life right now. God loves when His children pray to Him and come to Him for their needs or even their desires.

Day 18 - Questions to Ponder
1. *What do you want God to do for you in your life?*
2. *Are you grateful for what God has already done in your life?*
3. *How has God blessed you lately?*

Day 19

Ephesians 3:16-19: "...That He would grant you, according to the riches of His glory, to be strengthened with might through His Spirit in the inner man, that Christ may dwell in your hearts through faith; that you, being rooted and grounded in love, may be able to comprehend with all the saints what *is* the width and length and depth and height— to know the love of Christ which passes knowledge; that you may be filled with all the fullness of God."

The Christian life is not about storing treasure on Earth; it's about building the Kingdom of God. The riches that Paul talks about here are not riches on Earth but riches that God has. As you go on in your Christian life, you learn more about Him. You read the same Scripture, but the Scriptures become more meaningful and take on a different meaning as you read them at various stages of your Christian life. Thank God for the knowledge He gives you through the Scriptures.

Day 19 - Questions to Ponder
1. *What have you been learning about lately in your quiet time?*
2. *Are you able to share your faith regularly with others and share about what God is doing in your life?*
3. *Who can you talk with this week about God and what He has done for you?*

Day 20

> **Philippians 4:10-13:** "But I rejoiced in the Lord greatly that now at last your care for me has flourished again; though you surely did care, but you lacked opportunity. Not that I speak in regard to need, for I have learned in whatever state I am, to be content: I know how to be abased, and I know how to abound. Everywhere and in all things I have learned both to be full and to be hungry, both to abound and to suffer need. I can do all things through Christ who strengthens me."

Paul taught that we should learn to be content in whatever stage of life we are. If we have all we need and some of what we want, we should be content, but if we don't have all we need, we should also be content.

Also, this passage talks about helping others in times of need (in this case, it talks about Paul as he was a missionary). Think through people that you know are going through a hard time or need financial support. It's good to be able to help others in need, even if you aren't the most well-off person. God can use you to be a blessing to others.

Day 20 - Questions to Ponder
1. Are you content with what you have?
2. Do you know people who you can help?
3. Can you praise God if you have more than you have now? Can you praise God even if you have less than you have now?

Day 21

> **Colossians 1:10-12:** "that you may walk worthy of the Lord, fully pleasing *Him,* being fruitful in every good work and increasing in the knowledge of God; strengthened with all might, according to His glorious power, for all patience and longsuffering with joy; giving thanks to the Father who has qualified us to be partakers of the inheritance of the saints in the light."

We as Christians shouldn't stay at the level we were when we first became Christians. We should grow in Christ. Be thankful for where God has brought you and pray for God to give you more faith and trust in Him. Also, thank God for your salvation. Without Him, you and I wouldn't be able to get into Heaven, but through His grace, and His grace alone, we can enter those pearly gates and spend eternity with Him.

Day 21 - Questions to Ponder
1. *Are you at the same level of understanding or a higher level of understanding than when you became a Christian?*
2. *How can you get to a different level of your faith?*
3. *How can you help others in their walk of faith?*

Day 22

2 Thessalonians 3:3: "But the Lord is faithful, who will establish you and guard *you* from the evil one."

There is an enemy who is trying to get us to stumble and to get us to follow him. This enemy is Satan. While he isn't always the one active to get us to fall (many demons also work for him), God is faithful to protect us. Jesus showed through His trials how to be protected. Memorizing Scripture and reciting it when tempted is an excellent way to stop temptations.

Thank God for His faithfulness to protect us. He is the only one who can do so, and Satan's goal is to get everyone away from God. Pray that you will be able to overcome any temptation through God's strength that you are facing and are going to face.

Day 22 - Questions to Ponder
1. *Have you memorized Scripture?*
2. *What is your favorite Bible verse to think of when you are tempted?*
3. *Are you aware of Spiritual attacks in your life? What do you do when they come?*

Day 23

> **1 Peter 4:11:** "If anyone speaks, *let him speak* as the oracles of God. If anyone ministers, *let him do it* as with the ability which God supplies, that in all things God may be glorified through Jesus Christ, to whom belong the glory and the dominion forever and ever. Amen."

Use the gifts that God has given you. God gave you these Spiritual gifts for a reason, for you to help bring glory to His name. The Bible describes Christians as part of the body of Christ, and each body part has a function. The same with our Spiritual gifts. Christians work together as the body of Christ to accomplish God's Will on this Earth.

Do you know what your Spiritual gifts are? **1 Corinthians 12-14** talks about Spiritual gifts (it is one of the Bible passages that does). Talk with fellow Christians about what your Spiritual gift may be and pray that the Holy Spirit guides you to what your function is within the body of Christ. Thank God for this opportunity to be able to work with other Christians and fulfill His Will on this Earth.

Day 23 - Questions to Ponder
1. *Do you know what your Spiritual gift is?*
2. *Do you use this Spiritual gift for God's glory?*
3. *Are you thankful for the Spiritual gift(s) God has given you?*

Day 24

> **2 Timothy 4:17:** "But the Lord stood with me and strengthened me, so that the message might be preached fully through me, and *that* all the Gentiles might hear. Also I was delivered out of the mouth of the lion."

Paul was strengthened by God so that he could preach the Gospel of Christ. God has a purpose for you. If you haven't yet found your purpose, pray that God would guide you in helping to fulfill God's Will. Paul's purpose was to reach the Gentiles. Even though he had wanted to reach his own people, the Jews, God had other plans for him. What we want to do in life may be great, but if it's not what God's Will is, then we need to find out what His Will is for our lives.

Because of Paul's willingness to obey God's Will, God protected Paul and allowed him to do great things for God's glory. Paul gave all the praise to God, even when Paul and Barnabas were thought of as Hermes and Zeus, respectively, by a crowd in Lystra. Give God praise for who He is and for His protection in your life.

Day 24 - Questions to Ponder
1. Are you grateful for God's mercy in your life?
2. Do you know what God's Will for your life is? If not, seek Him out in prayer and reading the Bible to find out.
3. Will you obey God in what He wants you to do?

Day 25

> **Psalm 46:10:** "Be still, and know that I *am* God; I will be exalted among the nations, I will be exalted in the earth!"

God wants your neighbor to come to Christ. But, He doesn't just want your neighbor to come to Christ. He wants the whole world to come to Him. While the world is now becoming many people's neighbor (and emigrants from all over the world are moving to different parts of the world), this still doesn't excuse us from going to them as well to reach them with the Gospel. God wants everyone all over to come to Christ, so He sends people like you and like me to the uttermost parts of the world.

Is this you? If you are a disciple of Christ, then it should be you. Why not? The Great Commission is this: "'...All authority has been given to Me in heaven and on earth. Go therefore and make disciples of all the nations, baptizing them in the name of the Father and of the Son and of the Holy Spirit, teaching them to observe all things that I have commanded you; and lo, I am with you always, *even* to the end of the age.' Amen" (**Matthew 28:18-20**). This was a command to Jesus' disciples. Are we His disciples, too? Be thankful He will help us fulfill it.

Day 25 - Questions to Ponder
1. Are you Jesus' disciple?
2. Are you willing to follow Him?
3. Are you grateful He lets you be part of this?

Day 26

> **Matthew 11:28-29:** "Come to Me, all *you* who labor and are heavy laden, and I will give you rest. Take My yoke upon you and learn from Me, for I am gentle and lowly in heart, and you will find rest for your souls."

Sometimes we get so busy or so down that we get tired of doing everything we have to do. Isn't it good, then, that God calls us to rest? After all, He created the 7th day just for resting (and to worship Him together as the body of Christ). However, even more than that, He tells us to come to Him for rest. If you are tired of your day-to-day routine or have had hard times lately, God wants you to come to Him and pray for this rest that He offers.

Be thankful today that God will give you this rest that He has promised. He wants us to work for Him, but He also is a good Master and wants us to not overwork ourselves. Pray that He will give you this rest that you need, and thank Him for it.

Day 26 - Questions to Ponder
1. *Do you need rest?*
2. *Can you trust Him to give you the rest you need?*
3. *How thankful are you for this rest that He promises us?*

Day 27

> **John 16:33:** "These things I have spoken to you, that in Me you may have peace. In the world you will have tribulation; but be of good cheer, I have overcome the world."

Something that you may not expect in a book about thanksgiving is something about tribulation. Surprise! Here it is. Jesus says to be cheerful because He has overcome the world. Even in **Matthew 5**, Jesus calls the persecuted blessed. He says that their reward is the Kingdom of Heaven. Do you understand what this means? Our trials bring us closer to God. Why do they bring us closer to God? Because we have to rely on Him. When we are persecuted, we must start praying to God, which makes us closer to Him. **1 Peter 1:7-8** says, "In this you greatly rejoice, though now for a little while, if need be, you have been grieved by various trials, that the genuineness of your faith, *being* much more precious than gold that perishes, though it is tested by fire, may be found to praise, honor, and glory at the revelation of Jesus Christ." Our suffering brings God glory in the end.

Day 27 - Questions to Ponder
1. Are you thankful for the suffering God allows for His glory?
2. Are you aware of the outcome of your suffering?
3. Will you praise God, even through suffering?

Day 28

> **Romans 8:28:** "And we know that all things work together for good to those who love God, to those who are the called according to *His* purpose."

Yesterday was about how suffering brings God glory, so it is fitting to follow it up with **Romans 8:28.** All things, even suffering, "work together for good to those who love God, to those who are the called according to His purpose." God promises that everything, even our suffering, will turn out for good (if we are His). This means that, no matter what you are going through, God will make things turn around for the better, even if it is in Heaven when things turn around. You and I will spend eternity with the One who made us and who made everything.

Isn't this good news? Jesus has "overcome the world" (as we read yesterday from **John 16:33**). Our trials bring glory to God, and this should be what we live for, to see the glory of God shown to everyone around us, even to the ends of the world. My wife (Magda) and I chose **Romans 8:28** as our marriage verse. We even chose our wedding date as August 28 (since August is the 8th month) to remind us of God's promise to us.

Day 28 - Questions to Ponder
1. *Are you God's child?*
2. *Do you know your situation can become better?*
3. *Are you willing to trust, through prayer, that it will be better?*

Day 29

John 14:27: "Peace I leave with you, My peace I give to you; not as the world gives do I give to you. Let not your heart be troubled, neither let it be afraid."

Jesus says that we can turn to Him whenever we are troubled or afraid. We can have peace that is so powerful. Isn't this encouraging, that He will always be with us and that He will give us peace? However, we must accept that peace and not turn to worries or fear. God gives peace freely for those who ask for it. God knows everything that will happen to us, and we must trust Him to guide our lives. There isn't anything that surprises God because He knows everything and has made everything. Because of this peace we have, we learn to trust God more because He knows what He is doing. Ask God to give you this peace today and trust in His guidance through prayer and thanksgiving.

Day 29 - Questions to Ponder
1. *Where do you turn when you are troubled?*
2. *Who is available for you to turn to?*
3. *Are you thankful God is available 24/7?*

Day 30

> **1 Timothy 6:6-10:** "Now godliness with contentment is great gain. For we brought nothing into *this* world, *and it is* certain we can carry nothing out. And having food and clothing, with these we shall be content. But those who desire to be rich fall into temptation and a snare, and *into* many foolish and harmful lusts which drown men in destruction and perdition. For the love of money is a root of all *kinds of* evil, for which some have strayed from the faith in their greediness, and pierced themselves through with many sorrows."

The cure to worldliness is doing God's Will. There is no place in God's Kingdom for the love of money. Money is not what is wrong; it's the love of money that is wrong because it's a misplaced priority. When anything becomes an idol, it replaces God, even if the item can be good within reason. A desire for money will tempt people to do wrong things. If you have a love for money, pray that God will replace this love with more love for Him. God is the one who provides for us.

Day 30 - Questions to Ponder
1. *Do you have a love of money?*
2. *Are you content with what you have?*
3. *How thankful are you for what God has provided?*

Part Two: Small Groups Study Guide

The next few pages will have the Small Group lessons. You can use this section over an eight-week span of time, or you can combine two lessons each week to make it a four-week program. It is useful to use this book in small groups because you can hold yourselves accountable for being thankful. Also, as individuals, you can still follow the thirty-day section and talk about those devotionals each week in a Small Group setting.

Week One:
Thankful for Necessities

Read **Matthew 6:25-34**.

> "'Therefore I say to you, do not worry about your life, what you will eat or what you will drink; nor about your body, what you will put on. Is not life more than food and the body more than clothing? Look at the birds of the air, for they neither sow nor reap nor gather into barns; yet your heavenly Father feeds them. Are you not of more value than they? Which of you by worrying can add one cubit to his stature? So why do you worry about clothing? Consider the lilies of the field, how they grow: they neither toil nor spin; and yet I say to you that even Solomon in all his glory was not arrayed like one of these. Now if God so clothes the grass of the field, which today is, and tomorrow is thrown into the oven, will He not much more clothe you, O you of little faith? "Therefore do not worry, saying, 'What shall we eat?' or 'What shall we drink?' or 'What shall we wear?' For after all these things the Gentiles seek. For your heavenly Father knows that you need all these things. But seek first the kingdom of God and His righteousness, and all these things shall be added to you. Therefore do not worry about tomorrow, for tomorrow will worry about its own things. Sufficient for the day is its own trouble.'"

In this passage, we see that God will take care of our needs. Most of us probably have everything we need. We should be grateful for that. A lot of the world goes hungry every day, and there are thousands of people who die every day from starvation. This should drive us to be grateful and thankful to God for what He has given to us, and that He takes care of our personal needs.

The Bible says that instead of worrying about getting something we need, we should put our focus on God, and He will supply our needs. This doesn't mean we should quit our jobs and stop working, assuming that God will bring food, clothing, and shelter to us, but we should not worry when we do run into situations where we don't have all we need. Seeking God for our needs will bring us fulfillment because when we become Christians, we become God's children, and God takes care of His children.

Questions for Small Group Discussion – Week 1
1. *Have you been in a situation where it didn't look like you were going to have what you needed? How did you react to the situation, and how did the situation resolve itself?*
2. *For what can you be thankful?*
3. *What can you do to help others who are in need?*
4. *Do you have an accountability partner? If not, find one from your Small Group so you can be accountable in your prayer life.*
5. *Do you have any prayer requests for your Small Group?*

Close in prayer, thanking God for His daily provision.

Week Two:
Thankful For Your Spouse or Future Spouse

Read **Genesis 2:20-25**.

"So Adam gave names to all cattle, to the birds of the air, and to every beast of the field. But for Adam there was not found a helper comparable to him. And the Lord God caused a deep sleep to fall on Adam, and he slept; and He took one of his ribs, and closed up the flesh in its place. Then the rib which the Lord God had taken from man He made into a woman, and He brought her to the man. And Adam said: "This is now bone of my bones and flesh of my flesh; She shall be called Woman, Because she was taken out of Man." Therefore a man shall leave his father and mother and be joined to his wife, and they shall become one flesh. And they were both naked, the man and his wife, and were not ashamed."

We read in this passage that God created marriage between a man and a woman. He created marriage for companionship so that men would not be lonely, but He also created it so that men would have someone help them in their endeavors. Therefore, marriage should be a teamwork effort. If you are married, be thankful for your spouse and pray for him or her. If you are not married, thank God for your future spouse and pray for him or her.

God has given your spouse to you so that both of you can work together to accomplish the same goal. The Bible also says: "Two are better than one, because they have a good reward for their labor. For if they fall, one will lift up his companion. But woe to him who is alone when he falls, for he has no one to help him up. Again, if two lie down together, they will keep warm; but how can one be warm alone? Though one may be overpowered by another, two can withstand him. And a threefold cord is not quickly broken." (**Ecclesiastes 4:9-12**).

This passage does not only mean spouses; it also can refer to friends. However, a spouse does fulfill the role in that passage. A married couple should be a team, so in your own time, come up with ways you and your spouse can work together as a team to accomplish what God has given to you. Also, make sure to take time this week to show gratitude to your spouse.

Questions for Small Group Discussion – Week 2

1. *Can you come up with concrete ways to show gratitude to your spouse (you don't have to say answers, just as a group discuss how to show gratitude)?*
2. *If you are not married, what are ways you can show gratitude for your future spouse?*
3. *Do you have any prayer requests for your Small Group?*

Close in prayer, thanking God for your spouse or for your future spouse.

Week Three:
Thankful For Leadership

Read **1 Timothy 2:1-8**.

"Therefore I exhort first of all that supplications, prayers, intercessions, and giving of thanks be made for all men, for kings and all who are in authority, that we may lead a quiet and peaceable life in all godliness and reverence. For this is good and acceptable in the sight of God our Savior, who desires all men to be saved and to come to the knowledge of the truth. For there is one God and one Mediator between God and men, the Man Christ Jesus, who gave Himself a ransom for all, to be testified in due time, for which I was appointed a preacher and an apostle—I am speaking the truth in Christ and not lying—a teacher of the Gentiles in faith and truth. I desire therefore that the men pray everywhere, lifting up holy hands, without wrath and doubting."

When this passage says "kings and all who are in authority," it refers to government. It can apply to leaders in any of our types of governments: prime ministers, presidents, etc. Does this mean that governments cannot do wrong? That's not what this passage is saying. It is saying, though, that we should pray for everyone, including those who are in authority over the nation in which we live.

The Bible calls praying for leadership "good" because it is something that Christians should do, as well as praying to God for everyone else. **1 Peter 2:13-17** says, "Therefore submit yourselves to every ordinance of man for the Lord's sake, whether to the king as supreme, or to governors, as to those who are sent by him for the punishment of evildoers and for the praise of those who do good. For this is the will of God, that by doing good you may put to silence the ignorance of foolish men—as free, yet not using liberty as a cloak for vice, but as bondservants of God. Honor all people. Love the brotherhood. Fear God. Honor the king."

Questions for Small Group Discussion – Week 3
1. *Who puts leaders into place?*
2. *Can God change circumstances in the leadership of countries?*
3. *What role does prayer play in politics?*
4. *Have you recently prayed for leaders in your country?*
5. *Do you have any prayer requests for your Small Group?*

Spend time individually and in the small group in prayer for leaders in your country and for your government.

Week Four:
Thankful For Fellow Christians

Read **Ephesians 1:15-21**.

"Therefore I also, after I heard of your faith in the Lord Jesus and your love for all the saints, do not cease to give thanks for you, making mention of you in my prayers: that the God of our Lord Jesus Christ, the Father of glory, may give to you the spirit of wisdom and revelation in the knowledge of Him, the eyes of your understanding being enlightened; that you may know what is the hope of His calling, what are the riches of the glory of His inheritance in the saints, and what is the exceeding greatness of His power toward us who believe, according to the working of His mighty power which He worked in Christ when He raised Him from the dead and seated Him at His right hand in the heavenly places, far above all principality and power and might and dominion, and every name that is named, not only in this age but also in that which is to come."

God puts people in our lives for a reason. As a missionary and apostle, Paul met many Christians during his missionary journeys. He spent time in Churches where he wished he could spend more time. Since he couldn't always see them, he wrote letters to encourage them. He also prayed for the Christians that he met. He was very busy for this reason, but he also lived a full life of prayer, encouragement, and living his life for the Gospel and the furtherance of God's Kingdom. Without people like Paul, who knows where Christianity would be today!

Thank God for the fellowship that we have as believers. Thank God for the freedom that some Christians have to worship God, and pray for those Christians that are being persecuted for their faith in God (the same faith that you have). Pray for a continuance of the freedom of worship in places that have freedom of worship. Pray specifically also for Christians that you know.

Questions for Small Group Discussion – Week 4

1. *Why do we as Christians assemble as the body of Christ?*
2. *Does God put people in our lives for a reason?*
3. *What is Christian fellowship? What should it look like in the context of a Christian Church?*
4. *Do you have any prayer requests for your Small Group?*

Spend time in prayer individually and in your small group thanking God for fellow believers.

Week Five:
Thankful For Discipline

Read **Hebrews 12:7-11**.

"If you endure chastening, God deals with you as with sons; for what son is there whom a father does not chasten? But if you are without chastening, of which all have become partakers, then you are illegitimate and not sons. Furthermore, we have had human fathers who corrected us, and we paid them respect. Shall we not much more readily be in subjection to the Father of spirits and live? For they indeed for a few days chastened us as seemed best to them, but He for our profit, that we may be partakers of His holiness. Now no chastening seems to be joyful for the present, but painful; nevertheless, afterward it yields the peaceable fruit of righteousness to those who have been trained by it."

Who likes discipline? It's something that we consider taboo, something that we don't really like talking about as Christians, so why should we be thankful for it? As the passage you read says, discipline (or chastening) means that we are God's children. We don't get disciplined if we are not God's children.

In a human example, who does a father discipline: a random child or his own child? A man doesn't just go to the park and decide to discipline a child that isn't his own, does he? If he sees his child doing something that is wrong, he will chasten his own child.

This is the same with God; if we get chastened by God, this shows that we are His children. If we don't get chastened by God, we are not His children. Discipline is a sign of who is God's child and who is not. Therefore, it's something for which we should and must be thankful, even though it is not pleasant.

Questions for Small Group Discussion – Week 5
1. *Why does discipline exist?*
2. *Does discipline mean God loves us? Why or why not?*
3. *Is it possible to be thankful for discipline?*
4. *Do you have any prayer requests for your Small Group?*

Spend time in prayer individually and in your small group thanking God for His discipline of us.

Week Six:
Thankful For Everything

Read **Ephesians 5:15-21**.

> "See then that you walk circumspectly, not as fools but as wise, redeeming the time, because the days are evil. Therefore do not be unwise, but understand what the will of the Lord *is*. And do not be drunk with wine, in which is dissipation; but be filled with the Spirit, speaking to one another in psalms and hymns and spiritual songs, singing and making melody in your heart to the Lord, giving thanks always for all things to God the Father in the name of our Lord Jesus Christ, submitting to one another in the fear of God."

God loves you very much, and He wants you to be thankful for everything He has given to you and for every situation you find yourself in. God allows circumstances to change us and to mold us into who He created us to be.

God has given us many blessings, most of which we don't even realize or recognize as a blessing. Most likely, you are reading this in a building, with a roof over your head, with your church or with your church's small group. This means that He has provided your Church with a building, a place where you can meet. Also, you most likely have a place to stay at night, possibly a car, and other belongings.

As God's child, we are supposed to be grateful

for everything God has given to us. He has blessed us. Spend time in prayer individually and in a group and thank Him for the many blessings He has given you.

Questions for Small Group Discussion – Week 6
1. *Is it possible to be thankful in all situations?*
2. *What does being thankful in all situations mean in your daily life?*
3. *How can you show gratitude in the everyday parts of your life?*
4. *Do you have any prayer requests for your Small Group?*

Spend time in prayer individually and in your small group thanking God for everything that you can think of.

Week Seven:
Thankful For God's Protection

Read **2 Thessalonians 3:1-5**.

> "Finally, brethren, pray for us, that the word of the Lord may run *swiftly* and be glorified, just as *it is* with you, and that we may be delivered from unreasonable and wicked men; for not all have faith. But the Lord is faithful, who will establish you and guard *you* from the evil one. And we have confidence in the Lord concerning you, both that you do and will do the things we command you. Now may the Lord direct your hearts into the love of God and into the patience of Christ."

God's protection is all around us, but it may not always be evident, especially since we don't always know when we could have been in danger. However, whether we see it or not, it's there. Many examples are given throughout the Bible of God's protection for those in the Faith. Try to find some of these examples and, as a group, discuss these examples.

Now, as a group, discuss examples from your own lives of God's protection. Maybe you've had something from childhood or from your recent past where you know God's protection was evident.

Be thankful to God for His protection for you and for those in your group. His goodness is evident, and He protects us many times from possible accidents, catastrophes, and other forms of harm.

Paul had a lot happen to him during his lifetime, but God brought him through his various trials. If you are facing difficult situations right now, trust that God can bring you out of them. Put your life in His hands, as we're not in control of what happens to us anyway.

Questions for Small Group Discussion – Week 7

1. *How has God protected you in your life?*
2. *How can you be thankful for God's protection in your life?*
3. *What situations are you going through now where you have to trust God? Share with your group if you are comfortable doing so.*
4. *Do you have any prayer requests for your Small Group?*

Spend time in prayer individually and in your small group thanking God for His protection in your life.

Week Eight:
Thankful for Who God Is

Read **Job 38:1-11**.

> "Then the LORD answered Job out of the whirlwind, and said: 'Who *is* this who darkens counsel By words without knowledge? Now prepare yourself like a man; I will question you, and you shall answer Me. Where were you when I laid the foundations of the earth? Tell *Me,* if you have understanding. Who determined its measurements? Surely you know! Or who stretched the line upon it? To what were its foundations fastened? Or who laid its cornerstone, When the morning stars sang together, And all the sons of God shouted for joy? Or *who* shut in the sea with doors, When it burst forth *and* issued from the womb; When I made the clouds its garment, And thick darkness its swaddling band; When I fixed My limit for it, And set bars and doors; When I said, 'This far you may come, but no farther, And here your proud waves must stop!'"

Job went through a lot of things during his life, losing children, his health, his friends, and more. During his trials, he sought wisdom from his friends, who didn't always help him, but he eventually got to ask God why. God's answer had to do with who God is and that He controls everything. Job replies, "I know that You can do everything, And that no purpose *of Yours* can be withheld from You" (**Job 42:2**).

Thank God that He made you and that He knows everything about you. Also, thank Him that He is in control of every situation and that nothing takes Him by surprise. Begin to trust God more and more each day and through each situation.

Questions for Small Group Discussion – Week 8

1. Who is God to you?

2. What experiences lately have you had where you know God was working in your life?

3. Do you have any prayer requests for your Small Group?

Spend time in prayer individually and in your small group thanking God for who He is.

How Did This Book Help You?

I hope that this devotional has brought you closer to God and more willing and ready to bring Him your thanksgiving. I would love to know how this book has helped you. If you feel that this book has helped you grow Spiritually or if you have comments or questions, please feel free to write me at faithventuremedia@gmail.com to leave me a comment or a question. Also, please feel free to rate this book online.

If you have a Christian book you'd like to publish, we have a Christian book publishing package available for you to submit your book. Go to www.faithventuremedia.com/publishing for more info.

About the Author

Jeremy G. Woods was born in Huntsville, Alabama. He graduated from Grissom High School and from the University of North Alabama with a major in Marketing and a minor in French.

He currently lives in Târgu Mureş, Romania, with his wife, Magda, who is from Romania. Jeremy and Magda were missionaries in Romania (Jeremy moved overseas and met Magda while on the mission field), and they both currently write books and run a new company, FaithVenture Media. Jeremy and Magda are expecting their first child, due in January 2018. This is the 7th book Jeremy has published.

www.ingramcontent.com/pod-product-compliance
Lightning Source LLC
Chambersburg PA
CBHW060716030426
42337CB00017B/2888